YOUNG SAMURAI

W9-AHF-241

NEW EDITION with beginning TaeKwonDo basics

see page 45

By Merrill Matthews and Keith D. Yates

Printed in the United States of America

On this day, trouble was just waiting for one young mouse.

As he walked to school, two big, tough-looking mice came up and stopped him.

"Where ya goin', pip-squeak?"

"What's a matta? Are ya a fraidie-mouse?"

"Are you a mouse or a man?" they asked as they circled around him.

The young mouse trembled, afraid of these bullies, hoping he could get away.

"What'ya trying to do? High-tail it?" they taunted.

"You aren't goin' anywhere until you give us your cheese money," the leader demanded.

"But my mother gave me my cheese money for lunch," offered the young mouse softly.

"Give it to us or you're gonna feel more than just hunger pains," they roared.

When the young mouse got home that afternoon, his mother immediately saw that her son was scared and hungry.

"What's wrong, dear?" she asked him.

The young mouse paused and a tear came to his eye. He didn't want to tell his mother something bad had happened, but he didn't have to. She knew.

That night, after he finished his homework, the young mouse was watching a movie on TMC, The Mouse Channel, called "The Tail of the Seven Samurats." It was the story of seven courageous Samurai who helped a group of humble farmers defend their village against bandits trying to steal the farmers' cheese.

As the young mouse watched, he remembered what had happened earlier that day, and thought to himself, "If only I could . . . . "

The young mouse went to sleep that night wishing he had the courage of the Samurai.

The next morning as he was eating his Mice Crispies, the young mouse told his mother about his dream.

"I was a great Samurai," he said, "and defended a village against some mean old bandits."

"Well, son," said his mother, "I can't make you a Samurai, but I do have an idea."

"Let's find a martial arts school where you can take some lessons and learn how to defend yourself," said mom.

"Yeah," shouted the young mouse.

So they checked out schools of Tae Kwon Do ("the way of kicking and punching") and Judo ("gentle way") and Karate ("empty hand"). They finally settled on a school recommended by some friends.

When they arrived, a man in a white uniform welcomed the young mouse and his mother and began to tell them about himself and the dojo, a place where students learn the martial arts.

"I am the Sensei," he said.

"The word Sensei means 'teacher.'* I have learned the ways of the martial arts, and I will teach them to you."

"This is your uniform, which we call a *gi*," ** he explained as he handed it to the young mouse. "The white belt signifies emptiness. As you learn the ways, develop the skills and exemplify the spirit of the martial arts, your belt will change color."

The young mouse was very excited. "How long will it take me to get a black belt?" he asked.

"As long as it takes you to become ready," the Sensei responded. "But a black belt is not the goal, because even black belts have much to learn. Your goal is just to be the best student you can be and to try as hard as you can."

Sensei says — In karate it's the color of the belt, not the color of the skin that matters.

* Sensei (sen-say) really means "one who has gone before," but almost everyone thinks of a sensei as "teacher."

** Gi is pronounced "ghee."

When the class began, the students bowed to the Sensei, as the Sensei bowed back to the students.

After bowing, the young mouse joined the other students doing stretching exercises to prepare his muscles for the kicking and punching he would practice later. Then came the physical exercises to give his body the strength to do the karate movements with power.

And even though class had just started, the young mouse had already learned something: becoming a great Samurai would not be easy. But he tried as hard as he could.

The Sensei noted that the young mouse was trying very hard and was willing to do whatever he was asked. He recognized that the young mouse was already beginning to display the spirit of the martial arts.

"Very good," he told his new student. "If you continue working that hard, one day you will be a Master in the tradition of the great Samurai."

The young mouse's eyes grew wide with excitement: "That's what I dreamed about last night."

"Then I shall call you Young Samurai," declared the Sensei. "But the Samurai were not just good and courageous fighters; they lived the principles of the martial arts. As you come each day to take your lessons, I shall teach you those principles."

LESSON ONE

All the other kids were kicking so high that Young Samurai decided he would kick really high, too.

The young mouse hit the floor with a thud! What happened? All he was trying to do was kick as high as the other students. And the next thing he knew, he was on his back.

"Tell me what you did wrong, Young Samurai," he heard his Sensei say.

"I fell down," he squeaked back a little ashamedly.

"No, my young friend," replied the Sensei. "Falling down is only the result of what you did wrong. Now tell me what you did wrong."

"Well, then I don't know what I did wrong," Young Samurai offered.

"Then come with me and I will show you," said his Sensei with a smile.

Looking through the front window of the dojo at a beautiful blue jay perched on a very tiny limb, the Sensei asked Young Samurai, "Why doesn't that bird fall off its perch?"

"I'm not sure," responded the young mouse. "Is it because it is keeping its balance?"

"That's right," said the Sensei. "As long as the bird keeps its balance, it can perch on the smallest of twigs. You too must keep your balance in all that you do. When you lose your balance you fall, hurting yourself, and sometimes others also. Now go and practice your balance."

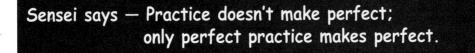

Sensei says — Practice doesn't make perfect; only perfect practice makes perfect.

LESSON TWO

At the beginning of class, the Sensei gathered the students around him to explain the importance of keeping their hands up when kicking.

"Students, you must always keep your face covered," Sensei said. "It is very easy to drop your hands when you begin to kick, but that leaves your head open so that..."

As Sensei talked, Young Samurai looked around the room, especially at all the weapons on the wall. There was a long stick called a "bo" and a shorter stick called a "jo" and two small sticks tied together called "nunchaku." And there was a Samurai sword!

Young Samurai recalled his dream of becoming a Samurai warrior fighting robber rats and...

"Young Samurai," he heard his name called out loudly.

"Yes, sir," the young mouse replied.

"Young Samurai, please tell the class what I have been talking about."

"Well, uh, I don't know, sir," he responded as his ears began to turn red.

"Young Samurai, at this moment you should be focusing on me, not other things. If you ever want to be good in the martial arts, you must learn to focus all of your attention on what you are doing. If you are distracted when faced by an opponent, he may defeat you before you can regain your focus."

Sensei says — The minute you lose your focus, you lose your battle.

LESSON 3

"Come here, Young Samurai," the Sensei said at the beginning of class. "I have something I want you to do."

"Yes, Sensei," the young mouse said as he ran to the front of the class.

"I want you to break this board in half," said Sensei.

"Break a board in half?" Young Samurai wondered aloud. "I can't break a board in half."

"How do you know?" returned the Sensei. "I will show you what to do."

Sensei explained to the young mouse how to hold his hand so that he could chop the board in half.

"Are you ready?" Sensei asked.

"I think so," Young Samurai answered.

He looked intensely at the board in front of him. He thought to himself, "I know I can do it. I know I can do it." He raised his hand, heard a karate yell come out of his mouth and the next thing he knew, his hand had broken the board — almost effortlessly!

Immediately, the young mouse felt a rush of pride.

"Did you see that? Did you see that?" he asked his fellow students. "Mouse, was that good! I am stronger than I thought!"

He looked at the Sensei for approval, but he didn't see it. Instead, he saw a frown.

"What's wrong, Sensei?" he asked. "Didn't I do well?"

"No," Sensei responded, "and it's not what you did, but what you thought. Breaking one board is a small accomplishment, yet you are filled with pride."

"Remember, if you can break one board, your next challenge is to break two. And if you can break two, then there are three boards. And if you can break three, then you must break a brick."

"While it is good that you can break one board, you must realize there are other difficult tasks to conquer. Balance your pride at accomplishing one goal with the recognition that you have many goals yet to achieve."

LESSON 4

Sensei had all the students sit in a circle. He called up the biggest and best student in the class, and then he looked at Young Samurai.

"Young Samurai, come here please," he said.

"Me?" squealed the young mouse out loud.

"Yes," the teacher replied.

Young Samurai got up and walked to the center of the class where Sensei and the other student were standing.

"I would like you to spar with this student," Sensei told him.

"Me?" squeaked the young mouse again.

"Yes," the teacher replied.

It was easy to see the alarm in Young Samurai's eyes. This student was much bigger, older and more practiced. How could the young mouse possibly spar with him?

"Why do you hesitate, Young Samurai?" Sensei asked.

"Well, he is much bigger and better than I am. Shouldn't I spar with someone more my size and ability?" he asked.

"No, you must spar with him."

The sparring match lasted only a few minutes, and the older student was clearly better. About all Young Samurai could do was keep his hands up to block the other student's punches and kicks.

When Sensei called on them to stop, the students bowed to one another and then to the Sensei and sat down.

After class, Sensei came up to the young mouse.

"Tell me, Young Samurai, when bullies look for someone to pick on, do they pick on someone their own size and skill level, or do they look for someone smaller and weaker?"

"They look for smaller and weaker mice," Young Samurai said.

"That's right. I could have put you up against someone your own size and skill level, but that's probably not the kind of mouse you will have to defend against."

"If you learn the principles of the Samurai, you will never pick a fight. So the only fights you are likely to be in are those that someone else picks with you. You will probably be smaller than your opponent."

"I didn't expect you to win the fight," Sensei continued, "but I did expect you to keep up your blocks so your opponent couldn't hurt you. And that's precisely what you did."

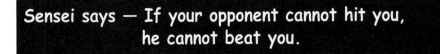

Sensei says — If your opponent cannot hit you, he cannot beat you.

LESSON 5

Young Samurai and another small mouse were talking to two of the older students about the class that day. After a few minutes, the two younger mice turned their backs to walk away and...

THUMP!!!

Young Samurai was lying on the ground and someone was on top of him holding and yelling at him! The young mouse tried to move his arms, but he couldn't. They were pinned to his side.

His face was pushed against the floor. He couldn't see and he couldn't breathe well, either.

He was scared! "What happened? Why did another mouse jump on me? Why am I being held down?" Young Samurai wondered.

At that moment the other student let go and got up. Young Samurai saw that he was one of the older students. Out of the corner of his eye, Young Samurai noticed that the other young mouse had also been jumped and was just getting up.

"Why did you do that?" Young Samurai demanded of the older mouse who had been holding him down.

The older mouse simply looked to the side and motioned Young Samurai to look also. Sensei was standing in the corner of the room watching everything that happened.

After brushing himself off, the other young student walked up to the Sensei, followed by Young Samurai.

"Why did you have them do that?" the other young student demanded. "You had them jump us."

"What have you learned here today, students?" Sensei asked.

"Never to trust anyone," whined the other young student. "You should punish them for jumping on us.

We could have been hurt."

"Well," said Sensei, "should I punish them for jumping on you, or should I punish the two of you for not being prepared?"

Then he turned to the other mouse, who was thinking about what had just happened. "Tell me what you have learned, Young Samurai."

"Um," said the mouse as he looked at the floor and thought for a minute, his tail waving back and forth.

"Expect the unexpected?"

"Very good," Sensei said. "Indeed, you have learned something today."

Sensei says — Always be on the lookout for enemies seeking to hurt you, both without and within.

LESSON 6

Sensei called Young Samurai and another student up to spar. They bowed to the Sensei and to each other and then they began.

Young Samurai was looking for an opportunity to try out a new kick he had recently learned when — POP! The other student kicked him — HARD.

They started again and Young Samurai thought he might try a punch this time when — WHOP! The other student hit him first — and HARD.

Young Samurai started to get angry. He thought that students were supposed to use control when they sparred. That meant you threw a punch or kick, but you didn't actually hit the other mouse. You stopped it so it didn't actually hit and hurt. But the other student had hit Young Samurai twice already.

Well, if a punch or kick wasn't going to do it, Young Samurai would try one of the throws he'd just learned.

THUMP!!

Before Young Samurai knew it, he was lying on the ground. The other student must have thrown him first. This made him angry.

Young Samurai got up with fire in his eyes and red on his ears. He wanted to get even. But Sensei stopped him immediately.

"What's the matter, Young Samurai?" his Sensei asked. "You look angry."

"Well, of course I'm angry. He just hit me twice and threw me on the ground and I'm gonna get even!" declared the mouse with a trembling voice.

"In that case," Sensei said, "the match is over. Bow to each other and have a seat on the floor."

After class, Young Samurai came up to the Sensei and asked, "Why did you end the match so soon? I wanted to teach him a thing or two."

"You had lost your self-control," the Sensei responded. "You would only lose again and you would have learned nothing."

"Young Samurai," the Sensei continued, "the martial arts are all about control. We control our kicks so we don't hurt other students. We control our attitudes for the same reason. One of the few things we can control in life is ourselves, yet very few mice achieve it. Self-control is the mark of every true martial artist. If you can master yourself, mastering anything else will be simple."

Sensei says — How can you control your opponent if you cannot control yourself?

LESSON 7

"Sensei, tell me once again why I have to learn these forms," Young Samurai pleaded as he started over again.

Sensei, who had been watching him intently, said, "These forms are called 'kata,' which means 'pattern,' and combine many of the moves you will need. Over the centuries, martial arts masters learned the kinds of blocks that work best, the best way to punch and kick, and the proper way to stand to stay in balance as they moved."

"They have combined all they know into these kata. Beginners learn simple ones, with very basic blocks and punches. More advanced students learn hard moves, punches and kicks. All force you to practice things you need to know."

"But they're so long," the young mouse complained. "I can never seem to remember all of the moves."

Young Samurai got ready to make his next move and ... he paused a minute. He went back to the last move and tried to make the next move again and....

"Oh, rats!" he said. "Sensei, I just can't learn this," and discouraged, he went to sit in the corner.

Sensei walked up to the little mouse and looked at him kindly. "Young Samurai, can you run faster now than when you were just born?" Sensei asked.

"Of course I can. It's all a baby mouse can do to move."

"But you did learn to walk, didn't you, one step at a time. And once you learned to walk, you learned to run, slowly at first, but you got faster. And that skill will last you the rest of your life."

"The process for learning these kata is the same. You have to take one step at a time."

"You know, Young Samurai," he continued, "kata is very much like life — a long series of different steps that become more difficult as we grow. Some people throw up their hands at life, too, and go sit in the corner. But that is not the spirit of the martial arts. You must take every step as it comes, learn from it and move on to the next."

LESSON 8

As the class began, Sensei called on Young Samurai and another student to come forward. He instructed the other mouse to grab Young Samurai, just as if he were an attacking bully.

"And, Young Samurai, when he does, I want you to defend yourself."

"Begin!"

The other mouse immediately reached out and grabbed Young Samurai by the arms. Young Samurai's eyes popped open as he frantically thought about how to respond. But his arms were already pinned.

"What am I going to do?" he thought to himself!

"Stop!" cried Sensei, and the other mouse let Young Samurai go.

"Well," Sensei concluded, "had that been a bully or a thief, you would have been beaten up or robbed."

"I tried to think of something to do," Young Samurai whimpered, "but by the time I thought of something, it was too late."

"That's right," Sensei said. "So what should you have done?"

"I don't know, Sensei, I think..."

"No, my young friend, that's precisely what you shouldn't do."

"I shouldn't think? But how will I know what to do?" asked Young Samurai.

"You will react. I have taught you many things. You have learned how to kick. You have learned how to punch. You have learned how to block someone else's kicks and punches and turn their moves to your advantage. You have spent hours practicing your kata, which teach you ways to respond to anything an opponent does. You have learned them well. Now you must have the confidence not to think, but to act. When an opponent tries to grab you, let what you know become what you do."

Young Samurai wasn't sure he understood, but he was willing to try again. As he waited for the next attack he thought, "I know what to do. Now I must let what I KNOW become what I DO."

As the other mouse reached for his gi, Young Samurai's hands shot up: one to deflect the other mouse's grab, the other hand went around the mouse's neck. In a moment, the other mouse was lying on the floor, and Young Samurai was standing over him looking down.

"Very good, Young Samurai," Sensei smiled approvingly. "You know it, you just had to have the confidence to do it."

Sensei says — Confidence comes not only from knowledge in the mind but through action in the body.

LESSON 9

As Young Samurai moved through his kata and other drills, he saw Sensei watching him closely. Was he doing something wrong?

As the Sensei approached, he said, "Young Samurai, your form is very good, but you have no power. You must add power to your moves or they will never work."

"I am trying as hard as I can, Sensei, but I am not very strong."

"And I didn't say you have no strength, I said you have no power. Do not confuse power with strength," Sensei replied.

"I'm not sure I understand the difference," Young Samurai said.

Sensei held out his hand. In it was a pebble.

"Take this pebble and throw it at the wall and see if it will go through," Sensei ordered.

Young Samurai was puzzled. He knew he couldn't throw the pebble hard enough to send it through the wall. But he threw it with all his might anyway — only to see it hit the wall with a slight clicking sound and fall to the ground.

"Now, Young Samurai, what would have happened if you had put the pebble into a cannon and shot it at the wall?"

"Well, I suppose the pebble would have blasted a hole in the wall," he responded.

"That's right," Sensei said. "But what's the difference? The pebble would still be the same size."

"Speed?" asked the young mouse.

"Yes," Sensei said. "A pebble is very small, but when it is traveling very fast, it has a lot of power.
You don't have to be strong to have power. You have to have speed. Power comes from how fast you do your technique."

"Few things are weaker than a pebble just lying on the ground. But shoot it from a cannon and few things are more powerful."

"That is true of mice, too, Young Samurai. The most powerful mice may often be the weakest. Their power comes from how they do what they do."

LESSON 10

"What are we going to learn today, Sensei?" Young Samurai asked.

Sensei looked at him and replied, "You must begin to learn what I cannot teach you."

"What does that mean, Sensei? If you can't teach it, how can I learn it?"

"Young Samurai, I can teach you how to fight, but I can't teach you when to fight. I can teach you how to defend yourself, but I can't teach you when to defend yourself or others. The greatest and most difficult lesson to learn is when to use your skills," said the teacher.

"Sensei, how will I know when I know?"

"You will know," said his teacher.

"Sensei, this seems really hard to understand."

"Yes, Young Samurai, it is hard to understand. Up to this point you have been training your body. Now you must train your spirit, and this is the hardest task of all."

"Your body will react as your spirit tells it. Your spirit will react based on the values you hold most dear. I can tell you that all mouse life is sacred, and that you should never hurt another mouse unless you absolutely have to. But unless you believe it, you will not live by it."

"Never forget, my young friend, value should be spelled 'val-you,' because it always ends in **you**."

THE BELT TEST

Finally, the day of Young Samurai's belt test arrived. After Sensei had all the students bow, the test began. Students started by showing how they could kick. Then they punched.

Next they performed their kata — and they could make no mistakes.

Young Samurai was a little nervous that he wouldn't remember it all, but he did. It came naturally.

The last part of the test was the sparring. Two students at a time had to battle it out on the floor, careful not to actually hurt one another.

When the test was all over, the students lined up as the new belts were awarded. And when his name was called...

"Young Samurai, step up and receive your new belt," Sensei said.

Everyone clapped as he walked to the front of the room. As he reached out to take his belt, Sensei smiled and said, "You have come a long way, my friend. But you've only taken the first step."

THE REAL TEST!

A few days after his belt test, Young Samurai was walking to school when he thought he heard voices.

"Give us your cheese money, kid!" said one rat.

"Yeah, if you don't we'll whip your tail!" threatened another.

Young Samurai recognized these voices! When he looked around, he saw the same two bullies picking on a field mouse. The field mouse was so afraid that he squeaked at the top of his lungs. But he was so tiny that he barely could be heard.

"What did Sensei tell me?" Young Samurai asked himself. "He said he could teach me how to fight, but he couldn't teach me when to fight. And he said he could teach me how to defend myself, but he couldn't teach me when to defend myself or others."

"Well, when you can help someone else who is being picked on, maybe that's when."

So Young Samurai walked straight toward the bullies. He focused on them, and as he came close he said confidently: "Leave that mouse alone."

"Who are you, pip squeak?" one of the bullies asked. Then he realized ....

"Oh, I know you. We took your cheese money a while back. Looks like we're in luck today. We're gonna get twice as much cheese money."

"No," said Young Samurai assertively. "You aren't getting any cheese money. And you're going to let that field mouse go."

"Oh," said the ringleader, "and who's gonna make us?"

"I will if I have to," Young Samruai replied, surprised that these words came out of his mouth.

One of the bullies reached out to grab him, but Young Samurai swiftly side-stepped so the bully tripped and fell on his face. The other bully swung a fist but Young Samurai grabbed his arm and gave it a slight twist, which sent the bully spinning to the ground.

Both of the rats got up ready to attack again. But they saw the look in Young Samurai's eye and they knew Young Samruai could hurt them if he had to. They looked at each other, then turned and ran off.

"Oh, how can I thank you?" the young field mouse asked shaking and wiping away his tears. "You saved me and my cheese money! And you did it all by yourself! You were so brave; I wish I were brave like you! Are you a master of the martial arts?"

Young Samurai thought for a moment about all he had learned — and about how much more he had to learn.

"No," Young Samurai replied, "I'm just a beginner."

The field mouse slipped his tiny hand into Young Samurai's hand as the two of them walked away.

And while Young Samurai had defeated the bullies alone, he didn't feel lonely at all.

The End

Beginning Tae Kwon Do Basics

The next few pages
show you the beginning moves
in American Nam Seo Kwan
(School of the Southwest)
Tae Kwon Do.

American Nam Seo Kwan was founded by Keith D. Yates, one of the authors of "Young Samurai". These are the beginning routines and requirements for the first three belt ranks in Nam Seo Kwan Tae Kwon Do. It usually takes about six or eight classes to learn all the moves for promotion from White Belt to Yellow Belt.

YELLOW BELT

Front Kick

Side Kick

Punching from Horse Stance

Nine-Step Blocking Pattern

Self-Defense from a:

Front Choke Hold

Hair Pull

Wrist Grab

Kicking is good to learn because your legs are not only longer than your arms, they are also stronger. Remember that balace is important when you kick because you are standing on just one leg instead of two.

Front Kick

Bring the kicking foot up to knee level and then SNAP the kick out and back. Hit with the ball of the foot (under the toes).

Side Kick

Bring the foot up to knee level, turn your hip slightly and then SNAP the foot out and back, hitting with the heel.

Punching from Horse Stance

Hit with the first two knuckles of your fist. Rotate the hand as you extend the punch. See how the hand at the belt is turned upside down.

Nine-Step Blocking Pattern (Ahop Palcek Mawki)

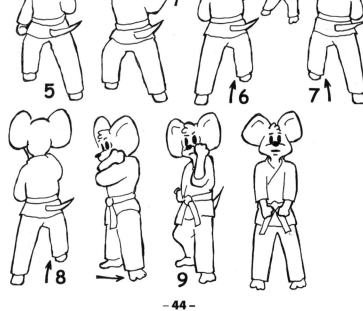

Self-Defense from **Wrist Grabs**

To escape you must twist your arm against his thumb.
If he uses two hands to grab you, you can also use two
hands by grabbing your own fist and twisting away.

Self-Defense from a **Front Choke**

Reach over through his arms and clasp your hands
together. Twist your shoulders and hips in the
direction of your top arm to force his hands off your
neck. You should step backwards after he lets go.
Then you could strike — or, maybe even better,
just ran away fast!

Self-Defense from a
Hair Pull

Immediately put your hand over the attacker's hand and hold it tight to your head so he can't pull on your hair and hurt you. Step back slightly and then kick or knee.

After one more session (usually six to eight classes), you will be elibible to test for the next rank — an Orange Stripe on your Yellow Belt. You will have to show the instructor that you remember all these moves.

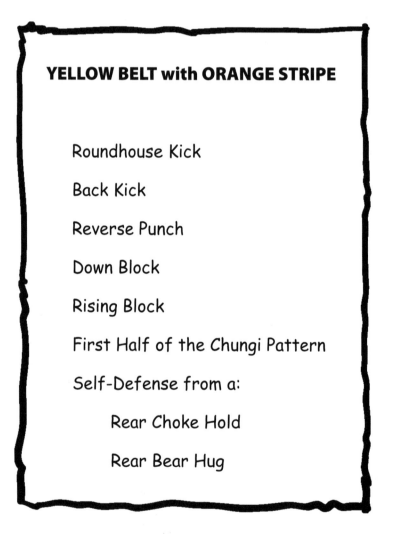

YELLOW BELT with ORANGE STRIPE

Roundhouse Kick

Back Kick

Reverse Punch

Down Block

Rising Block

First Half of the Chungi Pattern

Self-Defense from a:

Rear Choke Hold

Rear Bear Hug

Roundhouse Kick

Bring your hips around as you raise your back knee up high. SNAP your kick out hitting with either the top of the foot (instep) or the ball of the foot.

Back Kick

Pick your foot up to knee level and SNAP out the kick hitting with the heel.

Reverse Punch

The back hand snaps out and back, while the front hand stays up to block your face.

Now you are going to learn the Tae Kwon Do names (in Korean) for the basic blocks you did in the Nine-Step blocking pattern.

Down Block (Harden Mawki)

Fold the left arm on top and step out with a block over the extened leg.

Rising Block (Chukyo Mawki)

Bring the right arm high and the left arm down in front of your groin. Then step forward with a rising block over your head.

Chungi (Heaven and Earth)

This is the first half of the form. See page 59 for the second half.

Start in a ready position.

1. Step back and turn to your left into a low block.

2. Step with the right foot and punch to the center (solar plexus).

3. Move the front foot all the way around in the opposite direction and do a right-hand down block.

4. Step and punch with the left.

5. Move the front foot to the left 90 degrees and down block.

6. Step and punch with the right.

7. Move the front foot all the way around in the opposite direction and down block with the right.

8. Step and punch with the left fist as you yell.

This is the end of the first half of Chungi.

– 51 –

Self-Defense from a **Rear Choke**

1. Pull his arm down in order to get your chin tucked behind his arm (this keeps him from choking you).

1.

2. Rotate slightly and do a rear elbow. You can now run away or turn around for another strike.

Self-Defense from a **Rear Bear Hug**

1. Stomp on the attacker's foot.
2. Drop your hips and thrust your arms forward.
3. Elbow to the rear. Escape forward and follow up with another strike or run away.

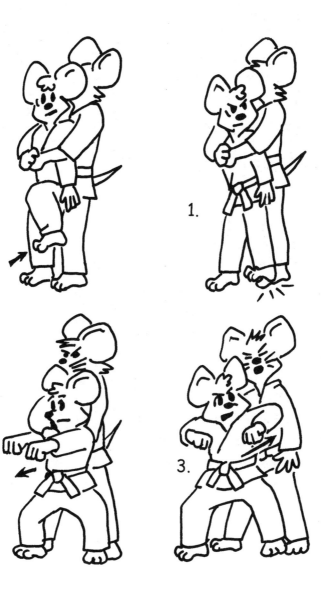

After another session you should be able to test for your Orange Belt. Remember that martial arts tests get harder as you advance in rank, so you must practice at home in between your regular classes.

ORANGE BELT

Front Leg Roundhouse Kick

Double Jump Front Kick

C - Punch

Inside Block

Outside Block

Second Half of the Chungi Pattern

Self-Defense from a:

    Rear Shoulder Grab

    Neck Pressure Points

Double Jump Front Kick

Do a regular front snap kick. But before you put the foot back on the floor, jump up with the other leg for another front kick.

Front Roundhouse Kick

This is similar to the back leg round kick, but you just pick up the front foot and snap it out and back.

C-Punch

Do a reverse punch low and then bring it back and out again (in a motion like a letter "c").

Inside Block (Arb Cheegi)

Bring the fists up facing outwards. Step forward and snap out the rear hand into a block. Notice that the hand crosses over the center of the face in order to block an attack to your nose.

Outside Block (Yop Mawki)

Fold the left hand underneath. Step out in a back stance (this is different from the other blocks where you had a forward stance) and block an incoming attack to the face.

Chungi (Heaven and Earth)

This is the second half of the form.

9. Fold the extended arm on the BOTTOM and turn to your left with an outside block.

10. Step with the right foot and punch to the solar plexus.

11. Move the front foot all the way around in the opposite direction and do a right outside block.

12. Step and punch with the left.

13. Move the front foot to the left 90 degrees and outside block.

14. Step and punch with the right.

15. Move the front foot all the way around to the opposite direction and outside block.

16. Step and punch with the left fist.

17. Step and punch with the right fist.

18. Step BACKWARDS and punch with the left fist.

19. Step backwards and punch with the right as you yell.

GOMON (finish) by stepping forward with the left foot. Bow.

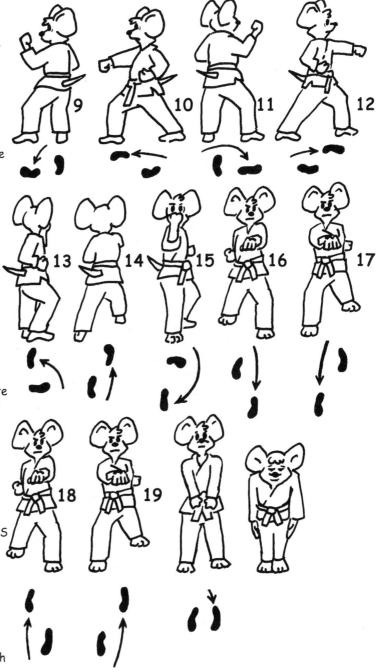

Self-Defense from a **Rear Shoulder Grab**

If someone grabs your shoulder, turn your head to see his hand. Turn towards his "pinky finger" with your whole body and block the arm off your shoulder.

The pinky is on the right side so turn to the right

Self-Defense showing **Pressure Points against a Choke**

Pressure points are areas where you can cause pain with little effort. One point is in the small hollow at the base of the throat. Other points are found under the ear and behind the ear lobes. Slight pressure is all you need.

A History of the Martial Arts

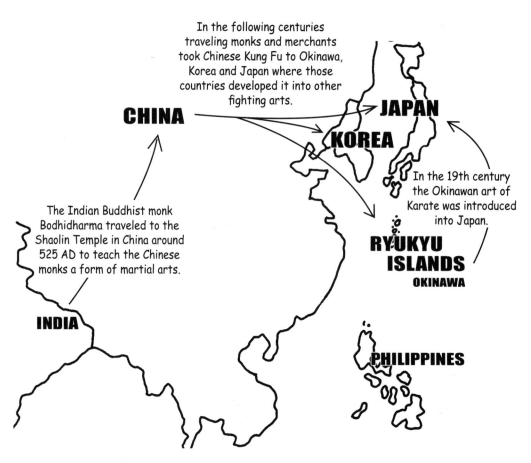

In the following centuries traveling monks and merchants took Chinese Kung Fu to Okinawa, Korea and Japan where those countries developed it into other fighting arts.

CHINA

JAPAN

KOREA

The Indian Buddhist monk Bodhidharma traveled to the Shaolin Temple in China around 525 AD to teach the Chinese monks a form of martial arts.

In the 19th century the Okinawan art of Karate was introduced into Japan.

RYUKYU ISLANDS
OKINAWA

INDIA

PHILIPPINES

Monks at the Shaolin Temple are said to have developed the earliest form of Asian martial art called Shaolin Boxing, which was later to become Kung Fu.

Chinese Kung Fu slowly made its way to Japan (helping to develop Ju-Jutsu), Korea (becoming the basis for Tae Kyon, and later Tae Kwon Do), and to Okinawa (which used the Chinese systems to build Karate).

Karate made its way from Okinawa to Japan in the 19th and early 20th centuries. The Japanese have developed several more styles of Karate in the 20th century.

Karate influenced the Korean art of Tang Soo Do which, along with Tae Kyon, became the basis for Tae Kwon Do, which was born in the 1950s.

Also in the 1950s, Tae Kwon Do came to America and joined the art of Karate, which had only arrived in the USA in the 1940s. The Americans developed their own approach to both Karate and Tae Kwon Do during the 1960s.

Martial Arts Glossary

American Karate — The generic name for an eclectic blend of techniques from traditional Asian systems combined by American instructors. Korean-based styles often use the term American Tae Kwon Do.

Dan (don) — A black belt rank (i.e., shodan means "first black belt").

Do (dough) — Literally the "way" or "path."

Dojo (dough joe) — A martial arts school. In Korean systems the term is "dojang."

Gi (ghee) — The karate uniform. In Tae Kwon Do they refer to the uniform as a "dobak."

Karate (ka rah tee) — Empty hand.

Kata (kah tah) — The training patterns. In Korean the term often used is "hyung" or sometimes "poomse."

Kia (kee aye) — A martial arts yell. Literally "shout with spirit." The Korean word is "kiap."

Kyu (queh) — Japanese term for the lower rank levels. In Korean, ranks below black belt are called "gup" levels.

Sensei (sen say) — A Japanese word meaning "one who has gone before," and indicating a mentor or teacher. The Korean term used for a martial arts instructor is "sabum nim."

Tae Kwon Do (tye kwon dough) — The way of kicking and punching.

American Nam Seo Kwan Tae Kwon Do

Jhoon G. Rhee — In 1956 Mr. Rhee arrived in Texas as the first Korean martial arts instructor to teach in the USA. He taught a style called Tang Soo Do (Way of the China Hand). Soon he adopted the brand new name for the Korean martial arts, Tae Kwon Do. Mr. Rhee is known as the "Father of American Tae Kwon Do."

Allen R. Steen — Mr. Steen was the first American to earn a black belt under Mr. Rhee. He did it in 1962. An International Karate Champion, Mr. Steen opened the very first martial arts dojo in the state of Texas (in Dallas). He is called the "Father of Texas Karate."

Keith D. Yates — Mr. Yates was one of Mr. Steen's original black belts (he earned it in 1968). A former champion and an author of many articles and books, he is known as the "Father of American Nam Seo Kwan."

Bruce Lee said that fulfillment lies not in the destination but in the journey. Good luck on your martial arts journey.